Miraculous Gopal

Adapted by Sita Gilbakian
Illustrated by Padmavati Devi Dasi

MANDALA
publishing group

From Ancient India come the mystical and enchanting stories of Gopal, the cowherder.

While living the life of a simple village boy, Gopal is actually God himself playing human. His adventures in the forests of Vrindavan bring both joy and amazement to those who hear them.

Endowed with limitless powers and riches, Gopal shows time and time again his greatest strength is his love and affection for his cows, friends and family.

One day Gopal saw his father, Nanda Maharaja, setting out golden bowls on the hillside.

"What are you doing?" Gopal asked. Gopal's father did not answer. Instead, he drew patterns on the ground with colored sand. So Gopal asked again, "Are you playing a game? Can I play with you?" Nanda Maharaja just continued arranging fruits and grains around a small altar. "Father please tell me what you are doing." Gopal's father shook his head. "I am very busy, please don't bother me." But Gopal wanted to know. He asked, "Is this a holy sacrifice to God?"

Nanda Maharaja finally stood up. He sighed and said, "Yes, this is a sacrifice for Indra, the king of heaven. He controls the clouds that bring us rain. Now please go and play somewhere else."

"Is Indra God?" Gopal asked. Nanda frowned and said. "Indra is one of God's helpers. Now please leave me alone."

"But why don't you just worship God?" Gopal asked. Nanda sighed again. "Because we need rain to grow fruits and vegetables. Without rain we will have no grain or grass for our cows to eat. We have to thank Indra or he might not send any more rain."

Gopal looked at Govardhan, the hill where the cows were grazing. "Why don't we just honor this hill instead?" he said. "What?" his father laughed. "And how will that make our Vrindavan Village prosper?"

"Well," Gopal said, "Our cows eat the green grass of this hill. Then we drink their sweet milk. The rivers water the trees. Then we eat their yummy fruits. And the bees make honey from the flowers. Don't you think that's all we need?"

Nanda smiled. "Yes, yes, tomorrow we shall hold another ceremony for Govardhan Hill. Now let me finish my ceremony for Indra."

"Oh no!" Gopal cried. "Please don't wait! Just take all the things you were going to offer to Indra and offer them to Govardhan Hill—right now." Gopal looked at his father and smiled sweetly. Nanda could not resist his dear son. He said, "All right. Just tell me what to do."

Gopal asked some villagers to cook a big feast. He asked others to feed the cows. He asked others to decorate the bullock carts. Everyone dressed in their finest clothes for a procession from the village to Govardhan Hill. They circled the hill, singing songs of thanksgiving. Everyone was very happy.

But not everyone was happy with the festivities. From his heavenly palace, Indra the God of Thunder, watched the Vrindavan villagers. He became very angry when he saw that they had stopped the sacrifice to him just because a little boy told them to. "They will suffer for this," he said. "I'll teach them to ignore me!"

Indra stomped around his palace. Thunder rattled from the ceilings, shaking the sky. Lightning flashed from Indra's eyes. In a loud voice he roared, "I'll show them how powerful I am! And I'll find a way to punish that rascal Gopal."

"Clouds!" Indra shouted. "Come here at once!" Hundreds of dark, threatening clouds flew into Indra's palace. "Yes Master. What is your order for us?" Indra roared, "Go flood the village of Vrindavan! I want it destroyed. Drown all the people. And make sure you drown all the cows too."

The clouds had never seen their master so angry before. Some of them were a little afraid of doing such a terrible thing. But Indra said, "Go right now. I will follow with my thunderbolts." So the clouds flew out of the palace and headed straight for Vrindavan Village.

Indra drove the clouds in a furious rage over Vrindavan Village. They hurled down streams of rain as sharp as arrows. They flung chunks of ice as heavy as boulders. They made the wind howl and shriek. Behind them Indra's lightning crashed, setting fire to the sky. His roaring thunder sounded like mountains shattering. Floods covered all of the fields and pastures of Vrindavan Village. Hailstones as big as rocks hit the bullock carts. Cows mooed in distress. Children cried and ran under their mothers' dresses for shelter. Indra screamed at his clouds, "Harder! Louder! Send more rain!"

Soaked to the bones, the villagers looked
for somewhere to hide from the terrible
rainstorm. The cows shivered and
trembled, trying to shelter their calves
beneath them. But there was nothing
anyone could do. They were far away from
their own homes. There was no escape
from the rain, hail, lightning and thunder.

Nanda Maharaja knelt down in a puddle of
water. He prayed, "Oh Supreme God, You
are so very kind to your devotees. You are
the most powerful. Please save us from
Indra's anger." All the villagers knelt
down, too. They echoed Nanda's prayer.
And waited for God to save them.

But it was not God in heaven who answered Nanda's prayer. It was little Gopal. He said, "Don't be afraid. I will protect all of you. I'll take care of Indra, too."

Nanda Maharaja laughed. "Don't be silly. You are just a little boy. There is no way you can stop this terrible thunderstorm. No one but Indra's master, the Supreme God, can save us now."

Gopal smiled at his father and all the Vrindavan villagers. "Believe me. I can really save you because I am Indra's master." Nanda and the other cowherd men giggled. They thought that Gopal was playing make-believe.

The villagers were still giggling when, using only one hand, Gopal picked up the whole hill of Govardhan. They could not believe what was happening. Gopal called to them, "Come and take shelter under this big umbrella."

But no one moved. They were afraid to go under the hill. They thought it would fall on their heads. They whispered to each other, "How is Gopal lifting this hill? Is it a magic trick? He's holding the big hill as if it were just a tiny mushroom."

"Come on," Gopal called to them. "Do not be afraid. I won't let the hill fall from my hand."

Gopal's father was the first one to trust
him. He said, "Let us take shelter of this
wonderful umbrella." Then the other
villagers went beneath the great hill.
Finally, the cows and their calves came,
too. But still the villagers worried. "Surely
this small boy cannot keep on holding
Govardhan Hill until the rain stops. Let us
take some of the weight off Gopal's little
finger," they said. So the men took the
sticks they used to prod the cows and
pushed them upward toward the bottom of
the heavy hill. Gopal laughed at their help.
"I can do this all alone, He said."

For seven days and seven nights Indra sent torrential thunder, lightning, hailstones and sleet, but the villagers were all safe and dry. Indra was very angry. "No one can withstand my powerful storms. Why haven't they all drowned? Why are they all so cheerful under that mountain?" Indra saw Gopal easily holding up the hill with his little finger. Then Indra looked at his storm clouds. They were all totally exhausted from blowing so hard and pouring so much rain all week long. "Enough," Indra ordered. "Stop all your gales. Stop all the showers."

Under Govardhan Hill the villagers noticed that the rain was stopping. "Listen! No more thunder!" the children said. "And no more lightning, either."

"Look everyone!" someone shouted, "The sky is clearing!" And so it was. The sun shone brightly and a beautiful rainbow arched in the sky. "Hurrah!" everyone cheered. "Indra has called off the dark rain clouds."

"Yes," Gopal said. "You can all go back to your homes now." One by one, the villagers and their cows left the shelter of the hill. Then Gopal carefully put Govardhan Hill exactly where it had been

The villagers placed a fragrant flower garland on Gopal. They cheered, "Hurray for Gopal!" The cowherd men lifted Gopal on their shoulders and carried him through the crowd. Everyone wanted to hug and kiss Gopal. They thanked him for saving them from Indra's angry rainstorm.

Gopal smiled and hugged them all. He knew that they did not know he was the Supreme Lord on earth. They thought he was just a little boy who somehow magically lifted a big hill. But one person realized who Gopal really was. From his palace in the clouds, Indra understood that Gopal was his Master.

Indra came down from the clouds. He wanted to apologize. "I am very sorry I sent floods and hailstorms to Vrindavan."

"I forgive you," Gopal said. "But why did you do it?"

"I became angry because you stopped the sacrifice that the cowherd men were going to hold for me," Indra answered. "But now I know that you are the Supreme God. I am only your servant." Indra bowed down before Gopal.

Gopal said, "Go back to your own planet, but always remember that you are only my agent. Neither you nor any of the other little gods is more important than your Lord."

After Indra left, Gopal walked back to Vrindavan Village with his brother, Balaram. Balaram asked him, "How did you manage to hold that big hill up for so long?" Gopal cuddled a calf in his arms. He said, "Did you forget who I am?"

"What do you mean?" Balaram asked. "You're my brother, Gopal. The son of Nanda Maharaja and Mother Yasoda."

"That's true," Gopal said. "But I am also the Supreme Lord, God of everything and everyone." Then Gopal winked. "But please don't tell anyone else. I want them to keep treating me like their little boy." Balaram smiled. "I'll keep your secret."

When Gopal and Balaram arrived home, their mother and sister were waiting. Yasoda gathered Gopal in her arms and smothered him with kisses. "You are such a brave little boy. Today you saved our whole village. If you had not lifted Govardhan Hill for us, we would have all been finished. It's a miracle how you were able to lift that heavy hill for so long."

"It was fun to do, Mother," Gopal said. Balaram started to say, "He could do it because...." Gopal gave his brother a nudge. Balaram winked at Gopal and finished saying, "....because Gopal is wonderful."

This exciting new line of beautifully illustrated children's books presents a charming and endearing narrative of the pastimes of Gopal.

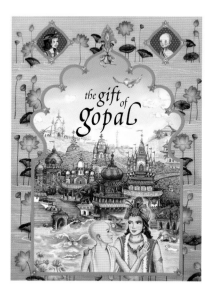

The Gift of Gopal

In this third part of the Gopal trilogy, Gopal has grown up and is Krishna, ruler of Dwarka. One of Gopal's childhood friends is encouraged by his wife to visit Krishna and asks him to alleviate their poverty. Upon seeing Krishna, this friend is overwhelmed with joy and is completely content, forgetting his request. However, Krishna manages to answer his friend's forgotten questions and desires.

$14.95 hardbound, 48 pages
Item 1213

Gopal the Infallible

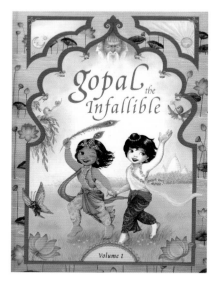

This tale recounts the pastime of Brahma's attempt to trick Gopal by kidnapping all of the cowherd boys and their cows and hiding them. Brahma waits for Gopal's reaction only to discover that the cowherd boys and cows are back where they belong. Gopal has tricked Brahma by expanding himself into replicates of his playmates. The cowherd children's parents are even fooled into treating Gopal's expansions (the Supreme Lord) as their own children. Brahma is the one who is bewildered in the end and surrenders to Gopal.

$14.95 hardbound, 48 pages
Item 1212

To our young readers
who are always eager
to hear the pastimes of
our friend Gopal.

Mandala Publishing Group
239C Joo Chait Road
Singapore 427496
65 342 3117 phone
65 342 3115 fax

103 Thomason Lane
Eugene, OR 97404 USA
541 688 2258 phone
541 461 3478 fax

1585-A Folsom Street
San Francisco, CA 94103 USA
415 626 1080 phone
415 626 1510 fax

mandala@mandala.org
www.mandala.org

Printed in Hong Kong through Palace Press International

ISBN 1-886069-18-2
Text © 1998 Mandala Publishing Group
Illustrations ® 1995 Attila Bakos and Agnes Vass